# Essential

# PowerPoint
# 2016

## Kevin Wilson

**elluminet Press**
www.elluminetpress.com

# Essential PowerPoint 2016

Publisher: Elluminet Press
Director: Kevin Wilson
Lead Editor: Steven Ashmore
Technical Reviewer: Mike Taylor, Robert Ashcroft
Copy Editors: Joanne Taylor, James Marsh
Proof Reader: Robert Price
Indexer: James Marsh
Cover Designer: Kevin Wilson

eBook versions and licenses are also available for most titles. Any source code or other supplementary materials referenced by the author in this text is available to readers at

www.elluminetpress.com/resources

For detailed information about how to locate your book's source code, go to

www.elluminetpress.com/resources

# Table of Contents

# About the Author

Kevin Wilson, a practicing computer engineer and tutor, has had a passion for gadgets, cameras, computers and technology for many years.

After graduating with masters in computer science, software engineering & multimedia systems, he has worked in the computer industry supporting and working with many different types of computer systems, worked in education running specialist lessons on film making and visual effects for young people. He has also worked as an IT Tutor, has taught in colleges in South Africa and as a tutor for adult education in England.

His books were written in the hope that it will help people to use their computer with greater understanding, productivity and efficiency. To help students and people in countries like South Africa who have never used a computer before. It is his hope that they will get the same benefits from computer technology as we do.

# Acknowledgements

Thanks to all the staff at Luminescent Media & Elluminet Press for their passion, dedication and hard work in the preparation and production of this book.

To all my friends and family for their continued support and encouragement in all my writing projects.

To all my colleagues, students and testers who took the time to test procedures and offer feedback on the book

Finally thanks to you the reader for choosing this book. I hope it helps you to use your computer with greater ease.

# Getting Around PowerPoint 2016

Microsoft PowerPoint allows you to create multimedia presentations that include animation, narration, images, and videos all from a library of pre designed templates or from a blank canvas.

PowerPoint can be used to create presentations for your up coming sales pitch, perhaps you are giving a lecture on a specific subject, teaching, or feeding back information in a meeting. All these can be enhanced using PowerPoint presentations as a visual aid.

To get your message across, you break it down into slides. Think of each slide as a canvas for the pictures, words, and shapes that will help you build your presentation.

You can create slideshows of family photos and holidays/vacations and send to friends.

You can also print out your presentation slides to give to your audience.

# Getting Started

You can start PowerPoint 2016 by searching for it using Cortana's search field on your task bar. Type in 'powerpoint'. Then click 'PowerPoint 2016' desktop app as highlighted below.

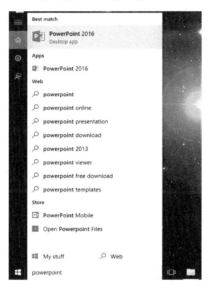

# Create a Shortcut

To make things easier, you can pin the PowerPoint 2016 icon to your task bar. I find this feature useful. To do this, right click on the PowerPoint icon on your taskbar and click 'pin to taskbar'.

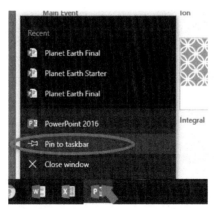

This way, PowerPoint is always on the taskbar whenever you need it.

# Chapter 1: Getting Around PowerPoint 2016

Once PowerPoint has started, select a template to open a new presentation or select blank to start your own. I'm going to go with mesh template.

Your most recently saved presentations are shown on the left hand orange pane below.

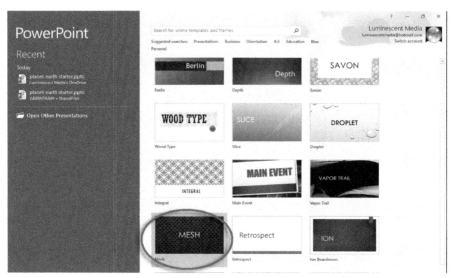

On some templates, you can choose colour schemes and styles for fonts and text. The mesh template has 4 different colour schemes which affect the colour of the text. Click on one and click create.

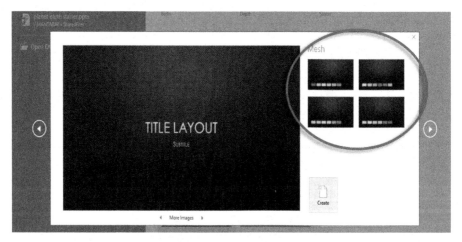

Lets take a look at PowerPoint's main screen. Here we can see, illustrated below, the screen is divided into sections.

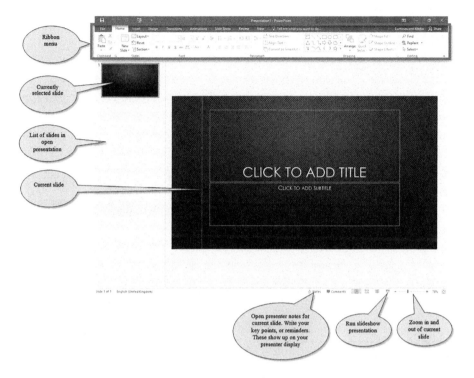

Down the left hand side, you'll see a thumbnail list of all your slides in the presentation, in the centre of the screen you'll see the currently selected slide you're working on, and along the top are your ribbon menus. This is where you'll find all your tools for creating your slides. Lets take a look at the ribbon menu.

# The Ribbon Menus

In PowerPoint, your tools are grouped into tabs called ribbons along the top of the screen. Tools are grouped according to their function.

## Home Ribbon

All tools to do with text formatting, for example, making text bold, changing fonts, and the most common tools for text alignment, and formatting.

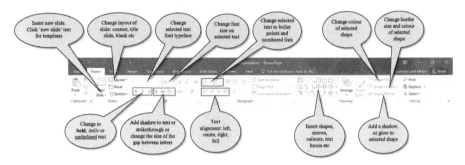

## Insert Ribbon

All tools to do with inserting photos, graphics, tables, charts, sounds, movies, etc.

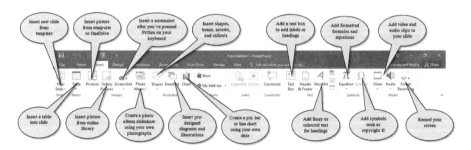

## Design Ribbon

All tools to do with the look of your slide, eg, the slide background.

## Transitions Ribbon

All tools to add effects to show as slides change from one to the next.

## Animations Ribbon

All tools to add slide transitions and adding effects to text boxes, images and headings.

## Slide Show Ribbon

All tools to do with setting up your slide show and running your presentation

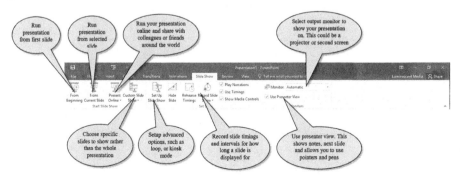

# File Backstage

If you click 'File' on the top left of your screen, this will open up what Microsoft call the backstage.

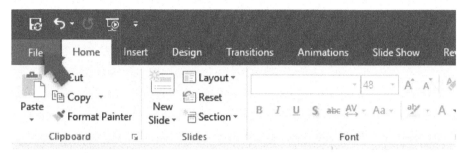

Backstage is where you open or save presentations, print, export or share presentations, as well as options, Microsoft account and preference settings.

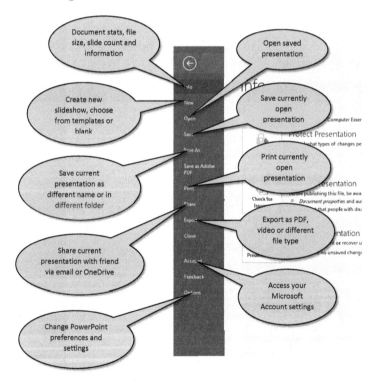

You can also change your Microsoft Account settings, log in and activate your Microsoft Office 2016, change PowerPoint's preferences and so on.

# Building Presentations

PowerPoint allows you to add photos, clipart, charts, diagrams, text, video, sound and animations.

You can add titles and photos to a slide, with animations and illustrations to get your point across.

In this chapter, we'll take a look at building a simple presentation, using one of the pre-designed templates commonly used in PowerPoint.

First thing we need to do is open a new presentation.

# Creating a New Presentation

PowerPoint has a wealth of templates and themes for all sorts of different types of presentations. When you start PowerPoint, you'll see a whole list of templates you can choose from.

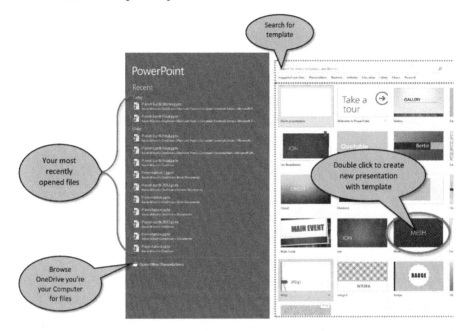

You can search for templates for the presentation you are creating. To do this, use the search field at the top of the screen.

To begin creating our presentation, for this example double click on the 'mesh' template. This will open up a blank presentation with this template for you to add your content.

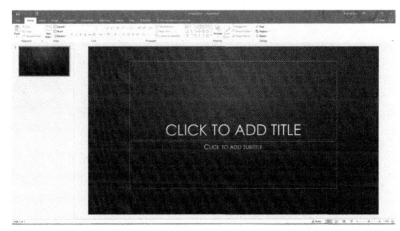

# Designing a Slide

Lets begin by adding the title to our first slide

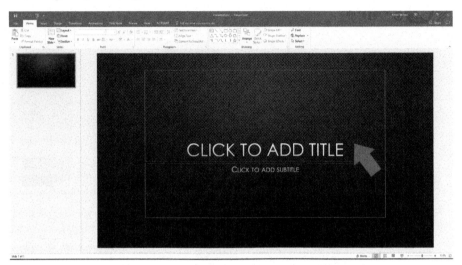

On your slide, click where it says 'click to add title'. This is a place holder for you to enter a title.

Enter the title 'Planet Earth'.

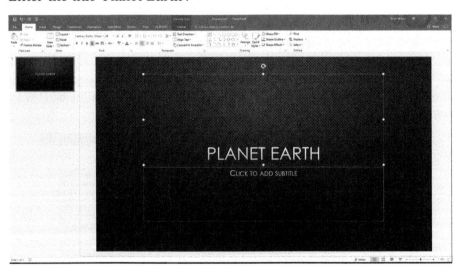

In this example, we won't be adding a subtitle, but you can add one if you want to.

Lets add some images to spice our title slide up a bit.

# Adding Images

You can add images or photographs from your computer, for example, photos you have taken. Or you can add images from Office's online library.

## From your PC

The easiest way to add an image to your slide, is to first find the image in your pictures library from file explorer. The icon is on your task bar.

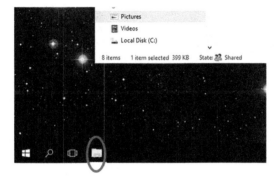

Open up your pictures library, then drag and drop the image onto your open slide, as shown below.

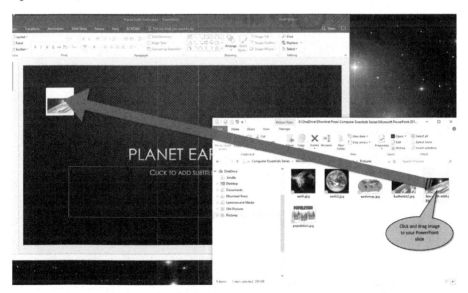

You may need to move your explorer window over to the side if it covers your PowerPoint presentation.

**21**

## Online Images

You can also add pictures from Office's online library. From your insert ribbon, click 'online pictures'

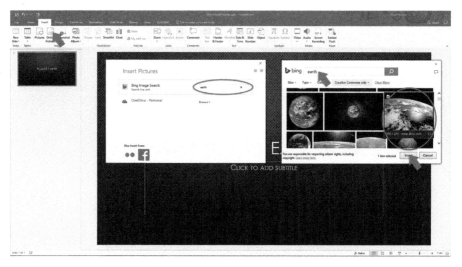

From the dialog box that appears, type your search into the Bing images field and press enter.

From the search results, click the image you want, then click 'insert'.

Now you can place your image and resize it to fit on your slide.

## Design Ideas

This is a handy new feature, and appears whenever your insert an image into your slide. PowerPoint will generate some ideas on how to arrange the image you have just inserted into your slide. If you see a design you like, just click on the thumbnail, listed down the right hand side.

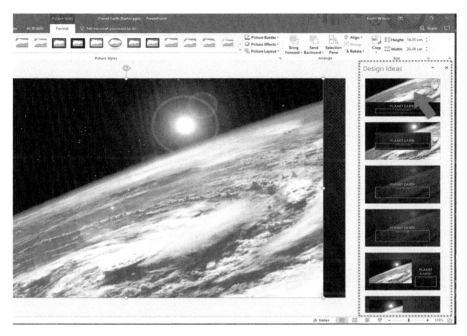

This is a quick way to format and arrange images on your slides.

If you don't choose any of the design ideas, you can arrange the image on the slide yourself.

## Resizing Images

If you click on your image, you will notice a border surrounding it.

In each corner and along the sides you will notice little white dots.

These are resize handles. You can click and drag these to resize your image.

To resize the image, click and drag the resize handles until the image is the size you want.

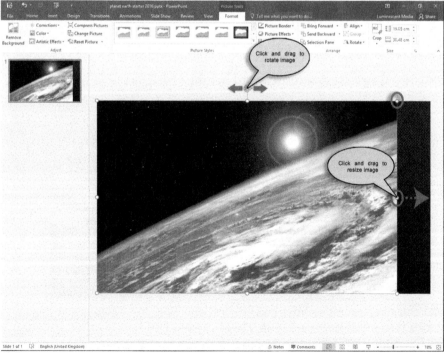

## Image Arrangement

You will notice that when you have resized the image, it covers the title. This is because PowerPoint constructs slides using layers. So the title "Planet Earth" will be on one layer, and the image will be on another layer. Now, because the image was inserted after the title, the image layer is on top of the title layer. We want the title layer on top.

We can adjust this by changing the arrangement.

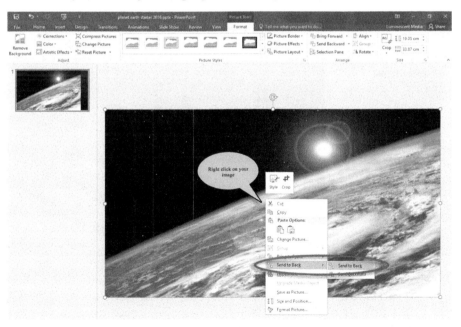

We want to put the image behind the title, so it's in the background on the slide. To do this, right click on your image and from the pop up menu, select 'send to back'.

**25**

You will see the image drop behind the text layer.

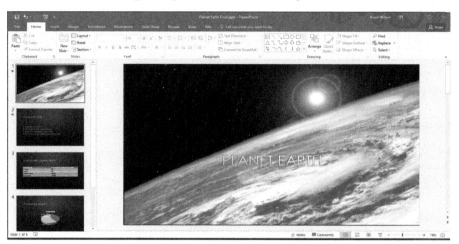

This is useful if you have a lot of images and text that you need to lay out on your slide.

You can now type the title 'Planet Earth' in the text box, and drag it to the desired position on the slide.

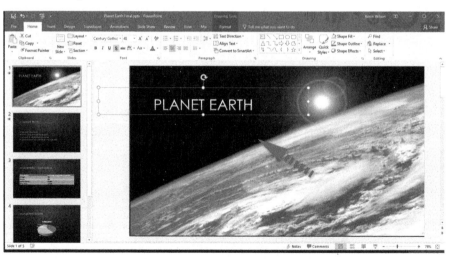

In my example, I'm going to put the title in the top left of the slide against the black. To drag the title text box, when you click on it, you'll see a box appear around the title text box. Click and drag the dotted line surrounding the title, to move your image.

# Adding a New Slide

To continue building our presentation we need additional slides to show our information.

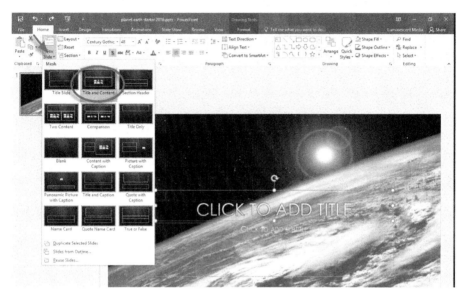

To add a new slide, go to your home ribbon and click on icon 'New Slide'. Make sure you click on the text to reveal the drop down menu.

From the drop down menu, select 'title and content' because we want a title on the slide but also we want to add some information in bullet points.

To add your text and titles, just click in the text boxes and start typing your information as shown below.

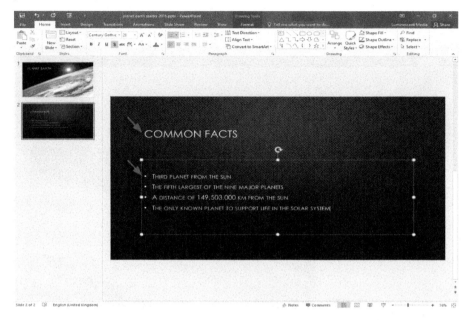

You can make text bigger by selecting it. Do this by clicking and dragging your mouse over the text so it is highlighted. Then click the home ribbon. From your home ribbon select the increase font size icon.

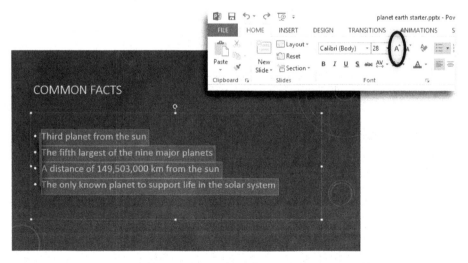

# Slide Masters

Slide masters allow you to create layouts and templates that are common to all your slides, so you don't have to make those changes to each slide.

Say you are creating a presentation and want a company logo on the bottom, you can add it to your slide master and the logo will appear on every slide you create.

To edit your slide masters, go to your view ribbon and click 'slide master'.

The larger slide listed down the left hand side is your master for all slides. The ones below are masters for individual slide templates such as 'title slides' or 'title and content' slides; these appear in the 'new slide' drop down menu. You can split them up so you can create templates for specific slides.

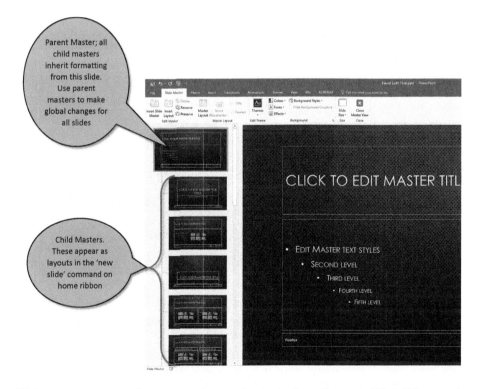

This way, you can have consistent layouts for all your title slides and all your content slides, without having to change the size of the title or position of text or the font every time you insert a new slide.

In this simple example, I am going to add the company logo to the bottom right of every slide. To do this, click on the larger master slide in the list on the left hand side.

Open your file explorer and navigate to your pictures folder, or the folder where the picture you want is saved. Click and drag your image onto the master slide.

You may need to resize your picture and position it in the correct place.

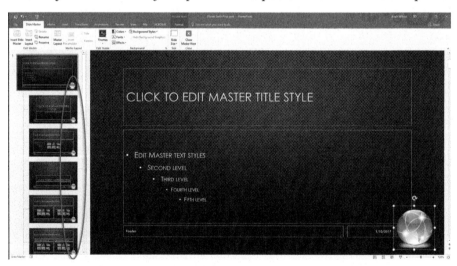

Notice, when you add the logo to the larger slide, it appears on the smaller slides too. This is because the smaller slides inherit their formatting from the larger slide; the larger slide being the parent master slide.

When you're finished click 'close master view'.

# Adding Notes

You can add speakers notes to your slides. These notes appear on the presenter view when running your presentation. They can also appear on printed handouts.

First reveal the notes pane. The notes pane is located at the bottom of your screen, but is usually hidden by default. To reveal the pane, click on the dividing line just above the scroll bar, illustrated below with the red arrow. You'll notice your mouse cursor change to a double headed arrow.

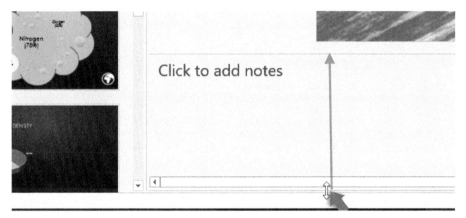

Then drag your mouse upwards to reveal the notes pane. You can add speakers notes, bullet points to help you when you're presenting.

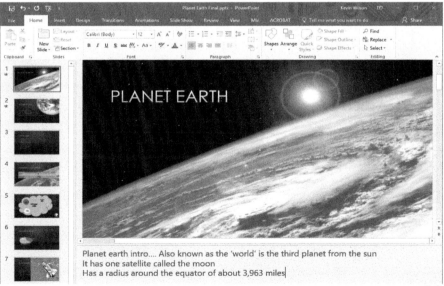

These notes will appear on your presenter view, when you run your presentation.

You can also include your notes in printed slide handouts. Go to FILE, then select print. Change the option, circled below, to 'Notes Pages'.

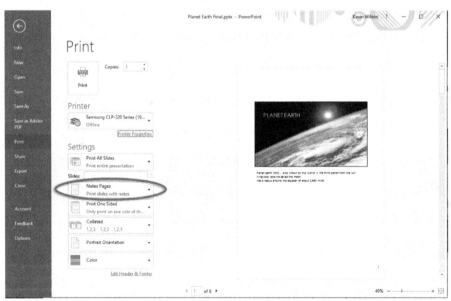

# Chapter 2: Building Presentations

# Adding Charts, Tables & Graphics

Microsoft PowerPoint has a wealth of objects, graphics, charts and tables you can use to illustrate your points.

You can insert tables and enter your data. You can format your data using colour, shading and borders to make your table look more visually pleasing.

You can present data in a wide variety of different types of charts, you can fully customise and edit these to your liking.

As well as add graphics and animations, transitions and shapes to bring your presentation to life.

Lets start by taking a look at presenting data in tables.

# Insert a Table

We are going to add a table to a new slide. In this example I have added a new slide with 'title and content'

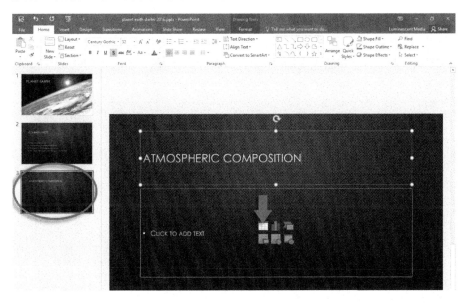

To add a table to this slide, just click the table icon from the template as indicated above. In the dialog box that appears, enter the number of columns and rows. This table is going to have 2 columns.

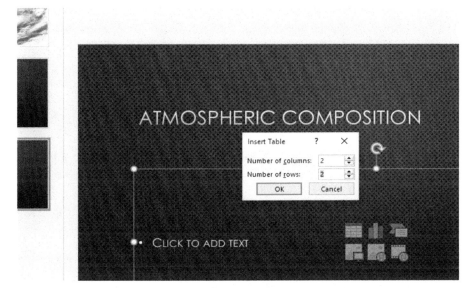

Once you have done that, enter the data into your table. Press the tab key to move between cells of the table. Don't worry about the number of rows, a new row will be inserted at the end of each row when entering your data; just press tab.

You can also insert a table directly. To do this, go to your insert ribbon and click 'table'.

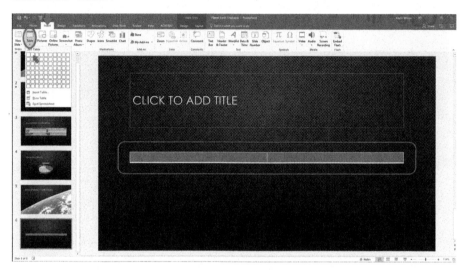

You can move or resize the table. If you click on the table, you'll notice an outline appear around the table with small dots around the edges. These are called resize handles and you can click and drag them to resize your table.

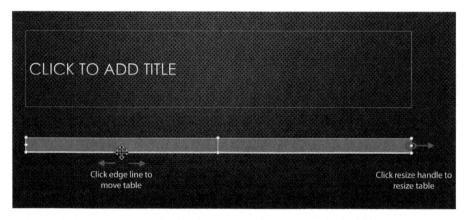

If you click on the edge line of the table and drag your mouse, you can move your table to the desired position on your slide.

# Formatting Tables

To do basic formatting, select the table with your mouse and click your design ribbon.

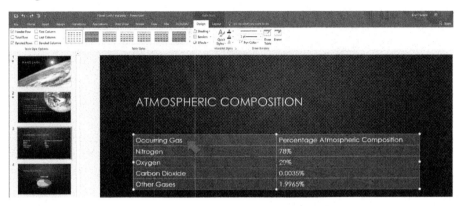

From here you can add some borders, change the shading or add an effect.

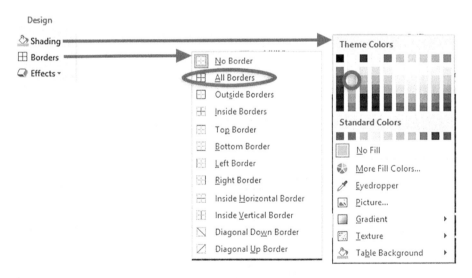

Click 'shading' and add a background colour to the cells. Since the slide is mostly grey, I'm going to choose a lighter grey to compliment the slide colour.

Then click borders, and select 'all borders' to put a border around all cells. You can also select individual cells or groups of cells and add borders to those to emphasise different parts of the table.

You can adjust the border thickness using the 'draw borders' section of the design ribbon. Click the drop down circled below and from the menu, select a thickness.

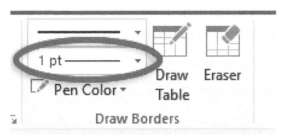

Finally click 'effects'. Select the type of effect you want; shadow or reflection effects work well. In the example, I am going to add a reflection effect to the table. Go down to 'reflection' and from the slide out, select the type of reflection effect.

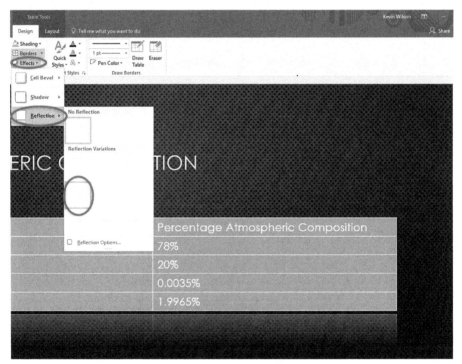

Try experiment with some of the other borders, shadings and effects using these controls.

## Table Themes

You can format your table using PowerPoint's pre-designed themes. This makes formatting your table quick and easy.

Click on the table then select the Design ribbon.

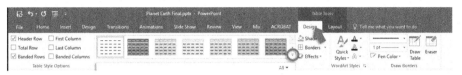

Along the centre of the Design ribbon you will see a number of pre sets. Click the small down arrow at the bottom right to expand the selections, circled above.

Click on a design to apply it to the table.

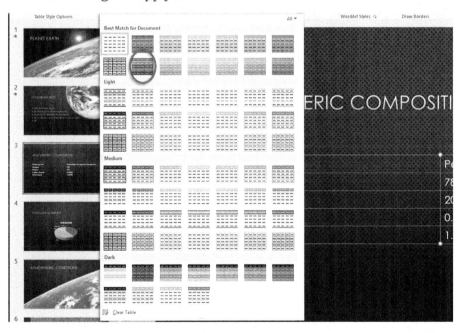

You can experiment with the designs by clicking on these and see how they look.

PowerPoint will automatically format the table using the colours and shadings in the themes.

# Add a Chart

We are going to add a chart to a new slide. In this example I have added a new slide with 'title and content'

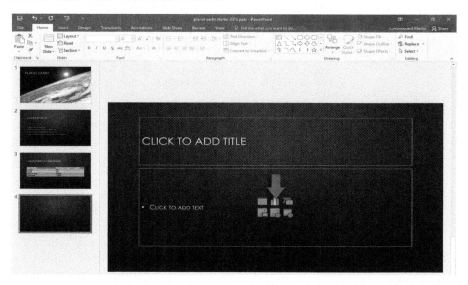

On the slide template, click the chart icon shown above. From the dialog box that appears, select the type of chart you want. In this example, I am going to use a nice 3D pie chart.

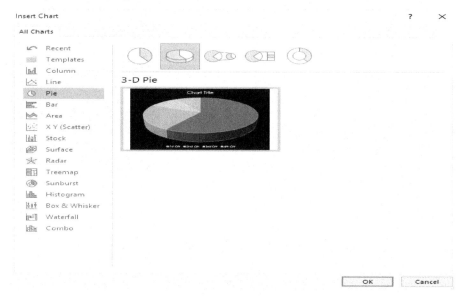

Click OK when you are done.

You'll see a spreadsheet like table open up where you can add some data. Enter the data in table shown below.

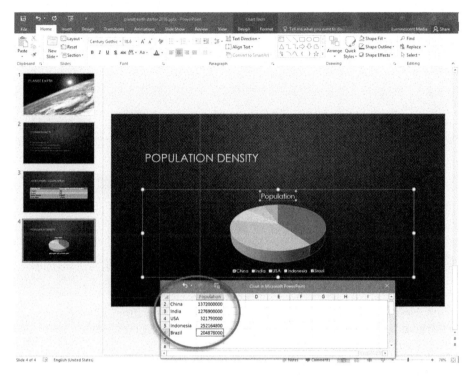

As you enter your data, you'll notice PowerPoint begins to construct your chart.

Remember when constructing your charts, **Column A** is the **X axis** on your chart, **Column B** is the **Y axis**.

# Formatting Charts

PowerPoint has a few chart formatting tools to take note of. First click on your chart to select it, you'll notice two new ribbons appear: design and format.

Lets have a look at the design ribbon. Note that there are actually two design ribbons. Make sure you select the ribbon under 'chart tools'.

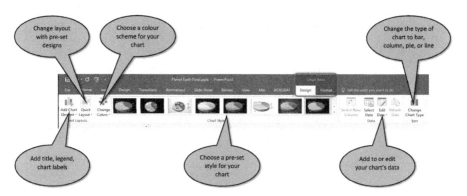

From here, you can do most of your basic chart formatting such as adding titles, editing your chart data and apply chart styles to make your charts look more visually appealing.

## Chart Titles

To a chart title, click on your chart and select the design ribbon. From the design ribbon, click 'add chart element'. Go down to 'chart title' and from the slide out click 'above chart'.

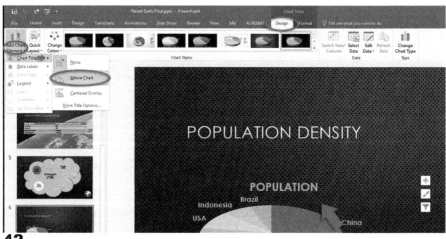

## Data Labels

Data labels are the labels that describe what the elements of the chart represent. You can either label each element of the chart or use a chart legend.

Click on your chart, then select 'add chart element' from the design ribbon. From the drop down menu, go down to 'data labels' and from the slide out, click 'data callout' or 'outside end'.

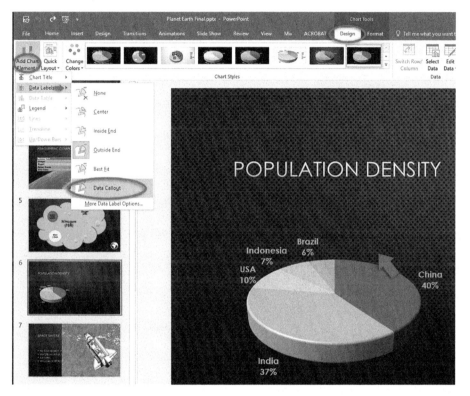

This tells PowerPoint where to position your labels.

# Chart Legends

Chart legends are good for explaining what the different parts of your chart represent.

To add a legend to your chart, click on your chart and select your design ribbon, then click 'add chart element'.

From the drop down menu, go down to 'legend' and from the slide out, click on the position you want the legend.

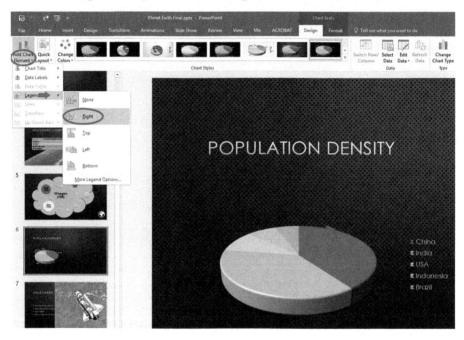

On the right is usually a good place.

## Edit Chart Data

To edit your chart data, click on your chart and select your design ribbon.

Click on 'edit data'. If you get a drop down menu, select 'edit data' again.

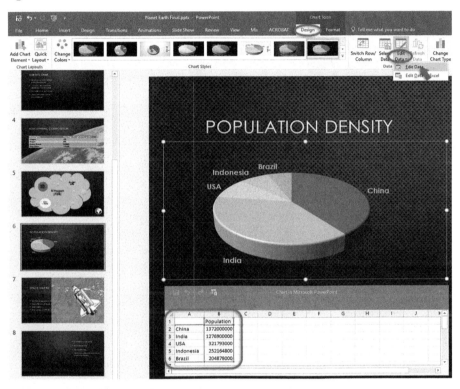

You'll see a spreadsheet like window open up with the data used to generate your chart.

You can edit the data or add to the data from here and PowerPoint will automatically update your chart accordingly.

## Chart Styles

You can style your charts pretty quickly using the style options on your design ribbon.

First, select your chart then go to your design ribbon. On the centre of your design ribbon, you'll see some chart styles. Click on one of the thumbnail icons to apply a style to your chart.

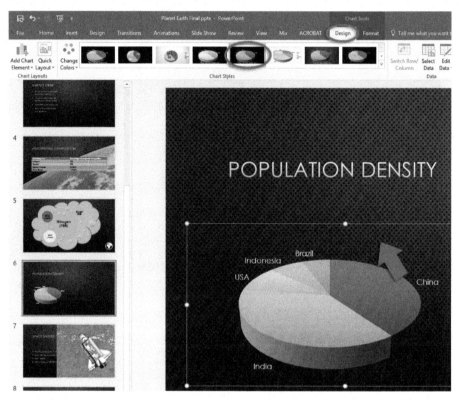

Choose one that matches the style of your slide.

## Chart Colour Schemes

You can also change the colour schemes; the colours used to represent the different data in your chart.

Sometimes the colours aren't as clear, so having the ability to choose different colour schemes helps with clarity and makes your chart stand out a bit more on your slide.

To do this, click on your chart and select the design ribbon. From the design ribbon click 'change colors'.

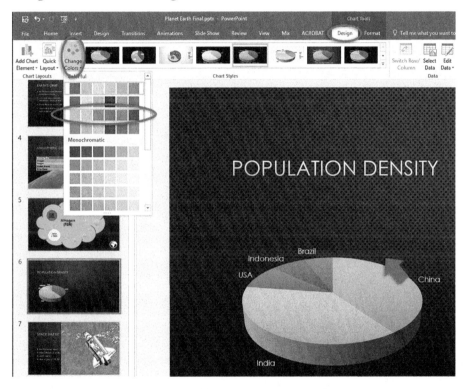

From the drop down menu, select a colour scheme that shows up your chart clearly and matches the colours of your slide.

# Adding Objects

PowerPoint has a large library of objects you can add to your slides. There are speech bubbles, circles, squares, lines, arrows, stars and a whole lot more to choose from.

## Shapes

To insert shapes, go to your insert ribbon and click 'shapes'. From the drop down menu you'll see a whole variety of shapes you can insert.

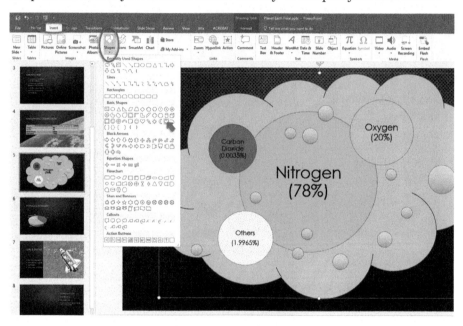

For this example, I am going to add a cloud shape to the atmosphere slide in my presentation. A cloud could represent the air, as this slide is illustrating. Inside the cloud or the air we could show the different gases.

So use the shapes to compliment and illustrate your slides.

You can change the fill colour of the shape and the outline. To do this, click on the shape and select your format ribbon.

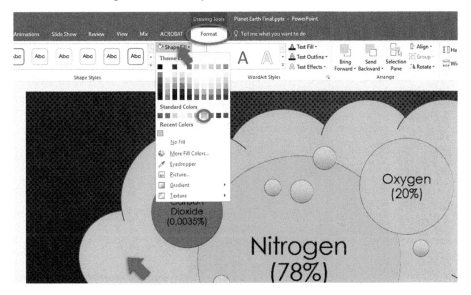

You can change the border of your shape in a similar fashion. Click your shape and from the format ribbon, select 'shape outline'.

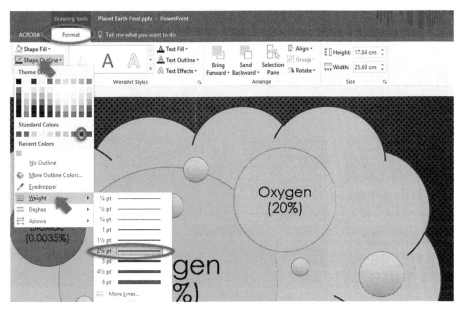

From the drop down, select a colour. Then go further down the menu and select 'weight'. This is the thickness of the border. From the slide out select a border thickness.

# Icons

Icons make nice little decorations and illustrations for your slides. You can use them as logos, or to illustrate a point.

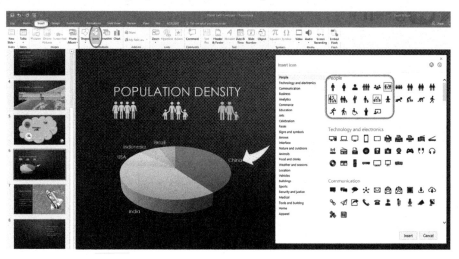

Here, I'm using an arrow to point to China; say for having the largest population and some icons of people and families to illustrate population.

You can change the colours of your icons. To do this, click on and icon on your slide, then from the format ribbon, select 'graphics fill'.

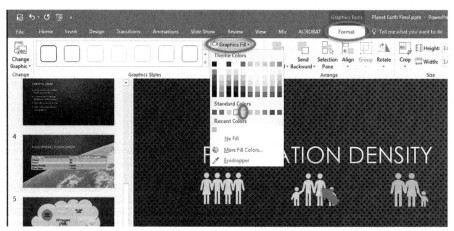

Select a colour from the drop down menu.

# SmartArt

SmartArt allows you to create info graphics, charts and so on. There are a lot of different types of pre-designed templates to choose from.

First, insert a new slide, or select the slide you want the SmartArt to appear. To insert SmartArt, go to your insert ribbon and click 'SmartArt'.

From the dialog box that appears, select a design. In this example, I am trying to illustrate the composition of gasses in the atmosphere, so I'm going to choose the circle design below that looks like gas molecules.

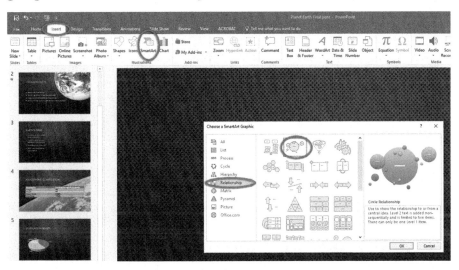

To edit the information, click in the text fields and enter your own data.

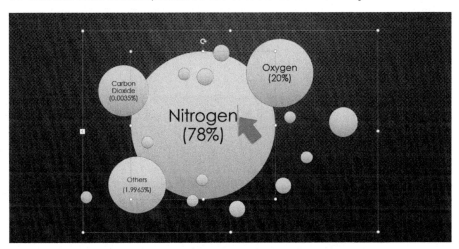

You can also change the design of the graphic. For example, change the layout, colour, add some shadows?

Lets change the colour of the 'other gasses' circle. To do this, click on the circle and select the format ribbon.

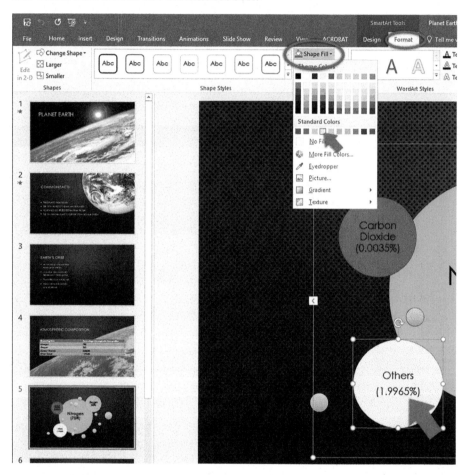

From the format ribbon, click 'shape fill'. Select a colour from the drop down menu. I'm going to colour this one yellow.

Try changing the colours of the other circles.

How about some shadows to separate the circles from each other and add a bit of depth to the graphic.

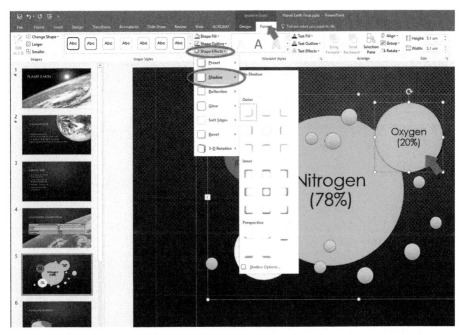

Do the same on some of the other circles. Try some of the other effects too. What about a glow?

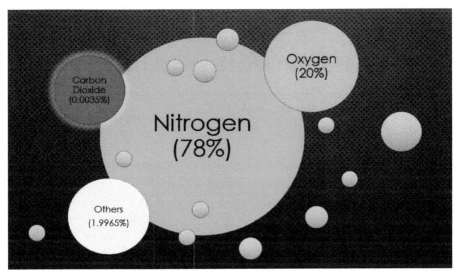

Experiment.

There are also some pre set styles that you can use to format your SmartArt graphic.

To do this, click on your SmartArt graphic and select your design ribbon.

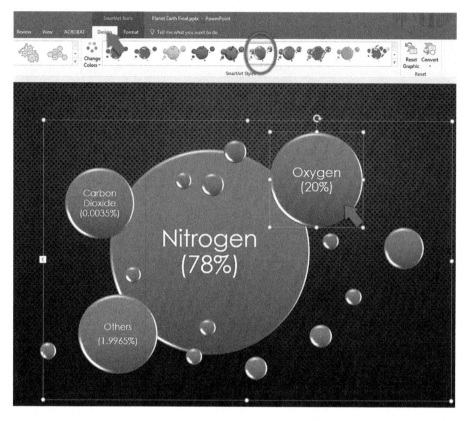

In the centre of your design ribbon, you'll see some SmartArt styles. Click on one of the icons to select the style.

# Adding Special Effects

You can adjust brightness and contrast, remove backgrounds, add animations and transitions between slides.

## Adjusting Images

Sometimes it helps to make some minor adjustments to your photographs or images to make them blend into your slide a little better. You can change the brightness, contrast and colours of the images. You can do all this by experimenting with the adjustments on the format ribbon.

For example. If we add another slide with the photograph of planet earth, the photo has a black background. We can make a few adjustments to this image to make it blend into the slide a little better.

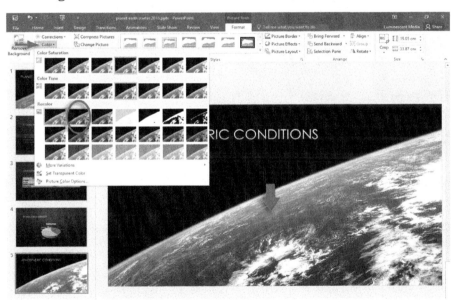

Click on the image on the slide and then click the format ribbon. On the format ribbon go to the adjustment section on the left hand side.

From the drop down menu, you can select 'color' if you want to change the colour blending of the image, eg select a grey tint to match the background theme of the slide.

You can also do the same for other corrections such as brightness and contrast. Do this by selecting 'corrections' from the format ribbon instead of 'color'.

**55**

## Removing Image Backgrounds

This works best on images that don't have complex or crowded backgrounds.

Instead of seeing the black background from the image, it would be better to use the slide background itself, rather than covering it up.

To remove the background, make sure your image is selected and click 'remove background' from the format ribbon.

This will highlight all the bits PowerPoint is going to remove from the image in dark purple. You will also notice a box surrounding the area.

Resize this box by clicking and dragging the resize handles until the box surrounds the area of the image you want to keep as shown above. In this case, around the earth.

Once you have done this click 'keep changes'.

Notice you can how see the slide background instead of the black background on the image.

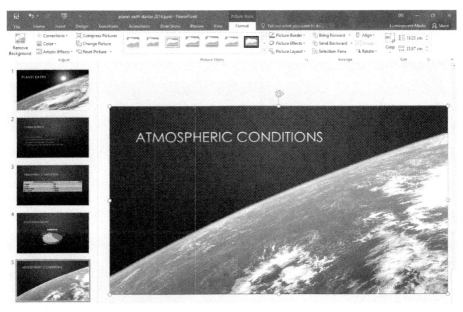

If your image is a bit more complex and doesn't have a solid background, such as this one of the shuttle, we'll need to tweak the purple mask a bit. After we align the mask box around the shuttle, if you look closely, you'll see that the purple mask has spilled over onto the edges of the wings.

You can mark these areas of the image you don't want PowerPoint to mask out. To do this, click 'mask areas to keep'.

On your image, draw a line across the bit of the image you want to keep. In this case, the edges of the wings. Shown below.

Once you've done that, you'll see the purple mask disappear from the edges of the wings.

Remember, anything highlighted in purple will be removed.

Click 'keep changes', when you're finished.

## Slide Transitions

A slide transition is an animation or effect that is displayed when you move from one slide to the next.

To add transitions to PowerPoint slides, click the slide you want to add the transition to, then go to the transitions ribbon.

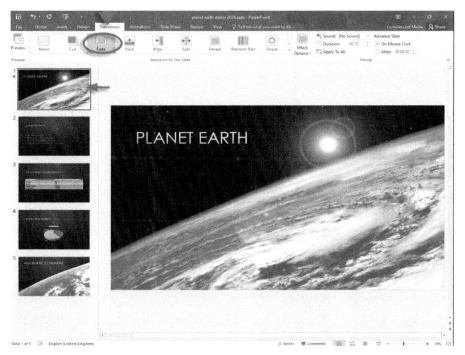

From the transitions ribbon, you can select from several pre set transitions. If you click on a transition, for example 'fade', this will apply the transition to the selected slide.

You can change the duration of the transition. The current duration is 0.7 seconds. If you want a slower transition, increase the duration. Try 1 or 2 seconds.

You can tell PowerPoint to wait for a mouse click to transition to the next slide, or you can make PowerPoint transition to the next slide after a set time. On the far right of your transitions ribbon, use 'on mouse click' to transition to next slide when you click the mouse, or un-check 'on mouse click' box and adjust the timer where it says 'after' with the length of time to display the slide.

To apply the transition to the whole presentation, click 'apply to all' on the right hand side of the ribbon.

# Animations

You can add animations to slides to move text boxes, make bullet points appear, animate shapes and so on. This can help to make your presentation flow so objects and text appear at the right time while you're presenting. Animation effects can also help to emphasise certain points.

## Effects

Looking at the slide below, say you wanted each bullet point to appear one at a time, instead of all at once.

You can do this by adding an animation to the text box. Click into the text box and select your animations ribbon.

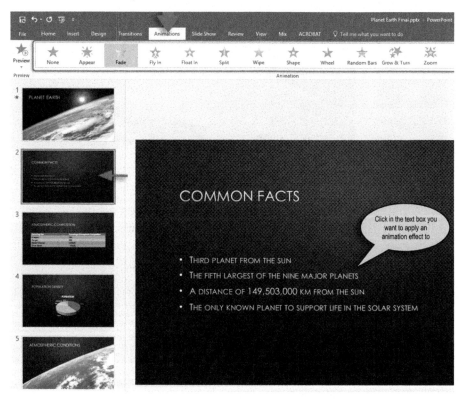

For this example, I am going to add a fade effect. To do this, select 'fade' from the animation pre sets circled above.

Try one of the other effects and see what happens. You can apply an effect, in the same way, to any object, photo, textbox, heading or logo.

**60**

## Motion Paths

A motion path is an animation effect that allows you to move an object such as a photo, shape or text box across the screen.

To create a motion path, first click on the object you want to animate. For simplicity's sake, I'm going to use a circle. Go to your animations ribbon, click 'add animation' and select 'lines' from the motion path section of the drop down menu.

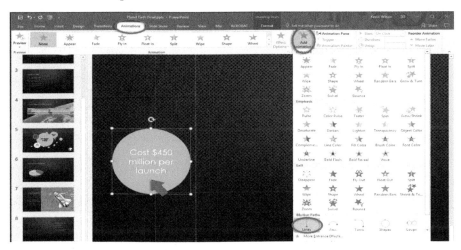

Now, if you look really closely, you'll see two very small dots on the light blue circles. One dot is green; this is the starting point. The other dot is red; this is the end point.

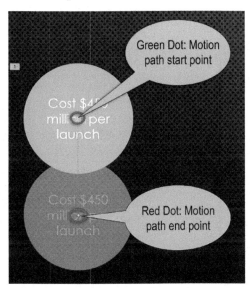

To create a motion path, you need to drag the green dot to the point you want the object to start at, then drag the red dot to the point you want the object to end up.

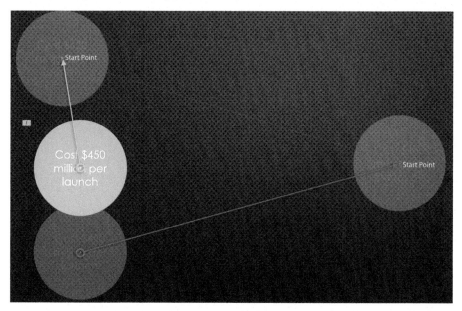

If you click 'preview' on the top left of your animations ribbon, you'll see the circle move left to right across the screen.

You can apply this effect to any object, textbox, photo or heading. You can also use different paths: arcs, turns or loops, and manipulate them in the same way, by moving the start and end points. Try an arc, to move the path, drag the resize handles on the box around the arc path.

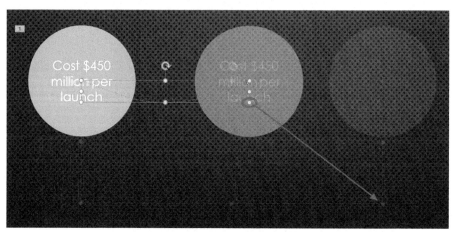

So you end up with something like this... you can see the motion path arc down then back up in a 'U' shape.

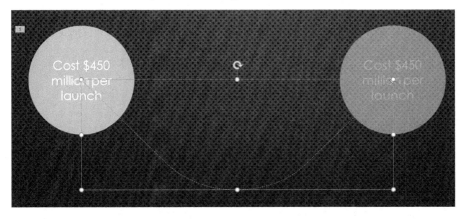

If the resize box disappears, click back on the motion path.

## Custom Motion Paths

You can also draw your own paths if you prefer. Click on the object you want to animate. Go to your animations ribbon, click 'add animation'. From the drop down menu, go right down to the bottom and click 'custom path'.

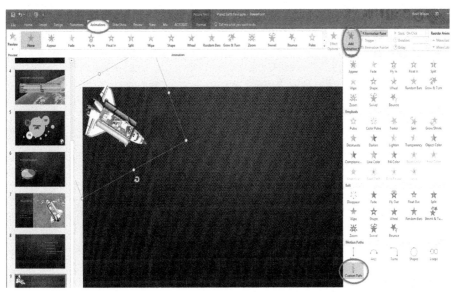

Now draw the path on the slide with your mouse. Highlighted below in red.

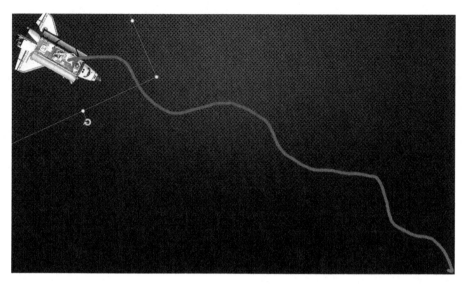

Double click on the position on the slide you want the object to end on.

Now, when you preview your slide, you'll see the ship fly to the bottom right corner.

If you double click on the path you have just drawn, you can make some adjustments to the speed and the timing.

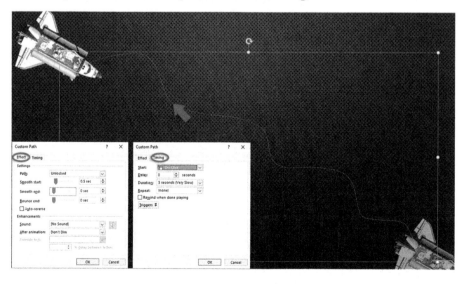

# Effects & Timings

You can adjust the timings. Set a 'smooth start' means the shape will start to move slowly then accelerate to full speed as it moves across the screen. Similarly 'smooth end' means the shape will gradually slow down as it nears the end of the motion path, rather than stopping suddenly.

'Bounce end' allows you to add a bounce effect to the shape when it gets to the end of the motion path - you can get the shape to bounce in a similar way to a ball bouncing on a hard surface.

Change these by entering the number of seconds into the boxes in the effect tab.

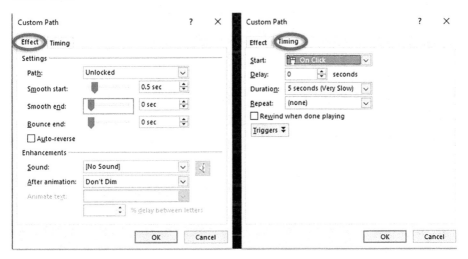

On the timing tab, you can set the trigger that starts the shape moving. Change this in the 'start' field. On mouse click is usually best to start your animation if you are presenting to an audience.

You can also set a delay before the animation begins with the 'delay' field, enter the number of seconds.

You can change the duration of the animation using the 'duration' field. This slows down or speeds up the animation on your shape.

You can set the animation to repeat a set number of times or until you click the mouse again, using the 'repeat' field.

## Animation Pane

With the animation pane you can view and manage all of the animations that are on the current slide. From here you can adjust timings and the order of your animations.

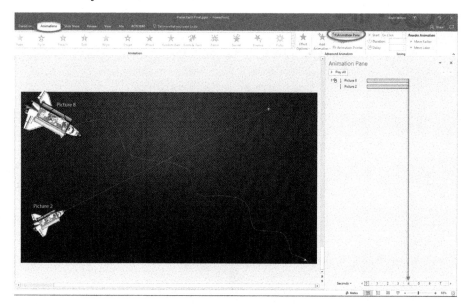

In this slide, we have two images; note their names, 'Picture 8' and 'Picture 2' as listed in the animation pane. Next to the object names in the animation pane, you'll see a blue bar. This is a timing bar and indicates how long the animation on that particular object is. The left hand side of the bar indicates the start while the right hand side of the bar indicates the end of the animation. You'll see a meter right at the bottom of the animation pane showing the number of seconds.

By default, PowerPoint will play the animations one at a time as listed in the animation pane. So for example, in the slide above, the animation on 'picture 8' will play, then when that animation is finished, the animation on 'picture 2' will start.

You can change the length of the animation by dragging the right hand edge line of the blue bar to the right, in the animation pane. You'll see the number of seconds on the end increase.

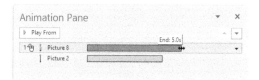

You can get the animations on the objects to start at the same time. On the animations pane, the first object in the list has a small mouse icon next to it, this means that the animation on that object will start when the user clicks the mouse.

Right click on the second object in the list and from the drop down menu, click 'start with previous'.

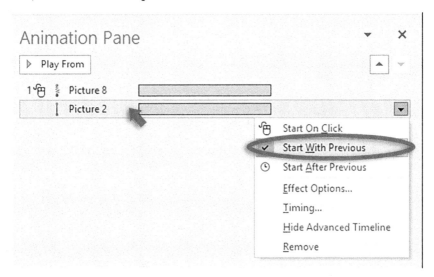

Now both animations will start at the same time. If you wanted 'picture 2' to start a bit after 'picture 8', drag the left hand edge of the blue bar next to 'picture 2', to the right. You'll see some seconds. This is the amount of time before the animation on this object starts. In this example, 'picture 2' will start 1.6 seconds after the user clicks the mouse.

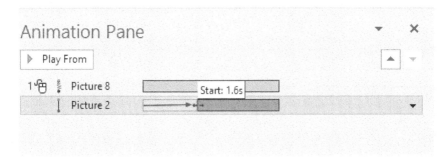

Picture 8 will start as soon as the user clicks the mouse.

This is useful if you have a sequence of objects that need to appear at different times during the slide animation.

# Chapter 4

# Using Multimedia

Now day's multimedia is very common place. You see video and audio everywhere; on websites, social media and music libraries.

PowerPoint allows you to add videos from YouTube online as well as your own recorded videos. You can embed these directly into your slide. Videos make great illustrations when used in a presentation.

You can also add audio and voice narrations to your slides.

You can create photo albums using either PowerPoint's own templates or your own design.

When you have your presentation ready, you can record narrations and timings, then export as a video for upload to YouTube or to send to a colleague/ friend.

Lets begin by taking a look at adding video files.

# Adding Video

You can add videos from your computer and videos from an online video sharing source such as YouTube.

## Add Video on your PC to a New Slide

To add a video to a new slide, click 'new slide' from your insert menu. From the drop down menu, click 'content with caption.

On the new slide, click the 'insert video' icon

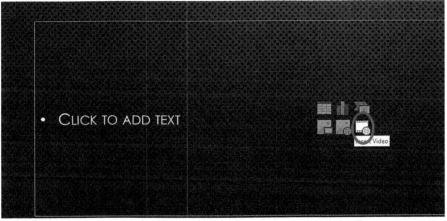

Select 'from a file', then from the popup dialog box, navigate to the folder on your computer where your video is saved. In this example, the video is in the 'videos' folder. Double click on the video you want to add.

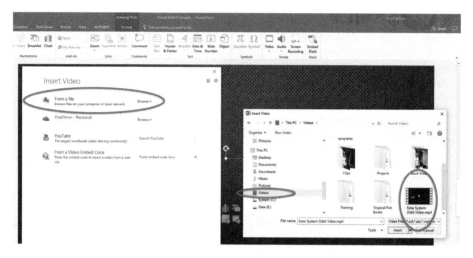

Add a title and some bullet points to your slide and here we go.

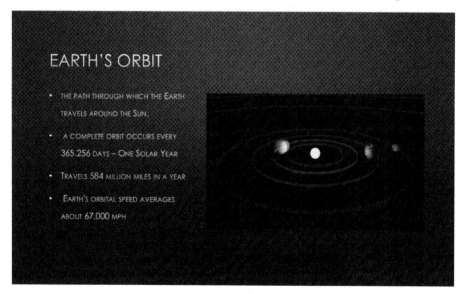

# Add video from your PC to an Existing slide

If you already have a slide that you would like to add video to, go to your insert ribbon and click 'video'. From the drop down click 'video from my pc'.

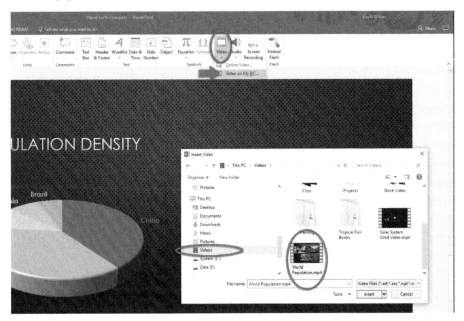

From the dialog box, double click the video you want to insert.

You may need to resize your video, if you don't want it to fill the screen. You can do this by clicking and dragging the resize handles on the edges of the video.

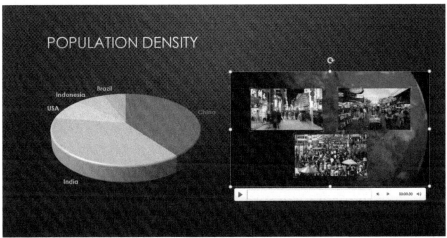

## Trimming Videos

You can trim videos to start in exactly the right place. You can't do this with online videos yet, but you can trim any that have been downloaded to your computer.

Click on your video and from the playback ribbon click 'trim video'.

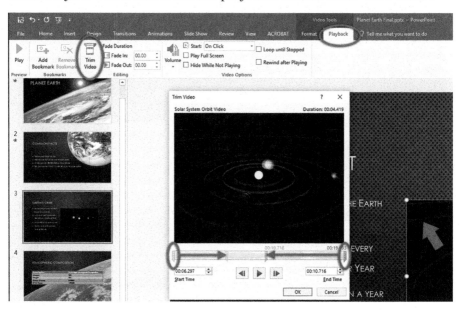

From the popup dialog box, drag the start point towards the right (indicated in red, above), to the point where you want the video to start. You'll see a preview of the video at the top of the dialog box.

Do the same with the end point. Drag the end point to the left (indicated in blue, above), to the point you want the video to stop.

Click OK when you're done.

## Online

You can link to YouTube videos from your slide. Insert a blank slide, then from your insert ribbon click 'video'. From the drop down menu select 'online video'.

From the popup dialog box, go down to YouTube, and in the search field type in what you're looking for. In this example, I'm looking for a video to go on my space shuttle page, so I typed 'space shuttle launch'.

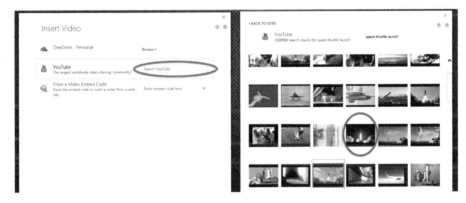

Double click on the video thumbnail in the search results to add the video to your PowerPoint slide. You might need to resize your video and move it into position on your slide. Add some information about it too.

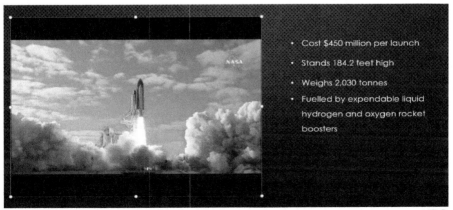

# Adding Sound

You can add audio files that contain music or voice as well as record your own audio.

## Recording Audio

To record audio, the first thing you should do is invest in a good microphone, especially if you intend to use your recordings as voice overs or links in a recorded presentation. This will vastly improve the quality.

The mic pictured below is a fairly inexpensive option.

This type of microphone will plug directly into a USB port on your computer or laptop with little or no configuration, which makes it ideal for PowerPoint presentations.

This comes in handy for recording narrations and presentations. We'll cover this a bit later.

# Audio on your PC

If you already have a slide that you would like to add audio to, go to your insert ribbon and click 'audio'. From the drop down click 'audio on my pc'.

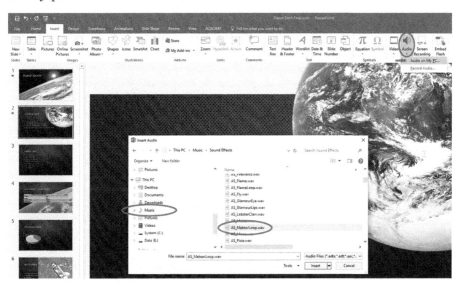

From the dialog box that appears, browse to the audio file you want to insert. In this example, my audio is stored in my music folder.

Your audio will show up as an icon on your slide.

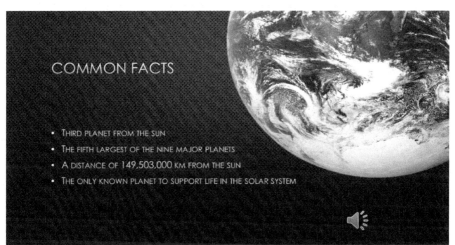

By default, you'll need to click the icon when showing your presentation to start the audio.

To change the audio settings, click on the audio icon, then select the 'playback' ribbon.

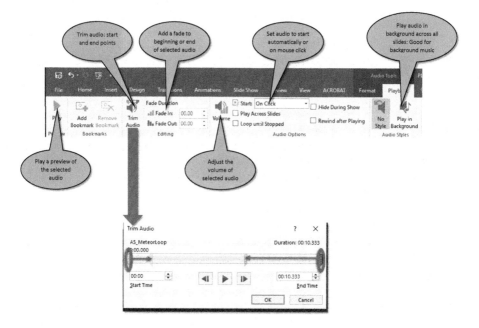

From here you can listen to a preview, trim the audio clip so it starts and ends in specific parts of the track.

You can add a fade in effect, so the audio fades in at the beginning and fades out to silent at the end, using the 'fade duration' options.

You can change whether you want the audio to play in one slide or across all your slides using 'play in background' option.

You can choose whether your audio plays automatically or if it starts when you click your mouse. You can adjust this using the 'start' setting on the audio options.

# Screen Recording

Screen recording is useful if you are demonstrating something on your computer, or training someone to use a piece of software.

First, select a slide or insert a new one, then select your insert ribbon. From the insert ribbon click 'screen recording'.

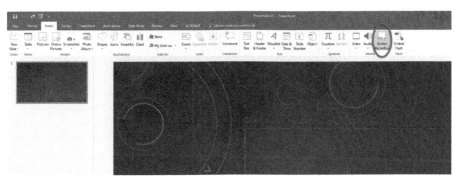

You will need to select the area of your screen you want to record. To do this, click and drag the selection box across the part of your screen to record, eg, click the top corner and drag your mouse across the screen, as shown below.

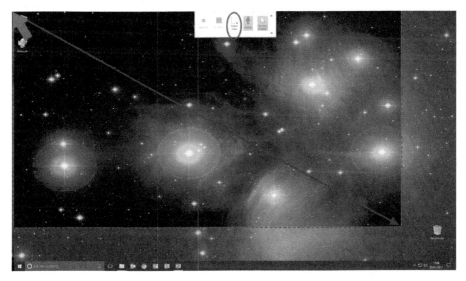

If you want the whole screen, click the top left corner and drag your mouse all the way to the bottom right corner.

When you have done that, click 'record' to start recording.

You'll get a 3 second countdown before you begin...

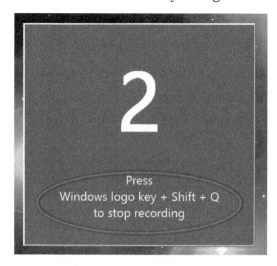

When the countdown hits zero, start the demonstration of what you're recording. PowerPoint will record your mouse clicks, applications opened and so on, within the area you selected in the previous step.

To stop recording, hold down Windows & Shift Key, then tap 'Q' - don't hold 'Q' down.

Your recorded screen video will appear in the selected slide. You may need to trim the screen recording because it's useful to remove the bits at the beginning where the control box is showing and at the end, so the screen recording just shows what you intended.

To do this, click on the screen recording video and from the playback ribbon click 'trim video'.

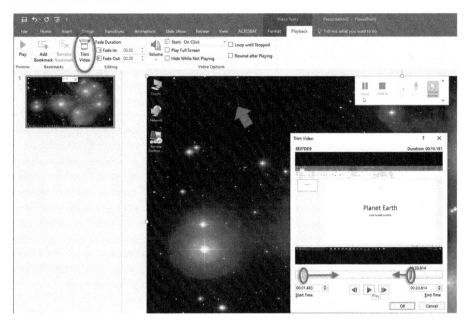

Now click and drag the beginning and end markers on the timeline to the points where you want the recording to start and where you want it to end.

Click OK when you're done.

# Recording Presentations

Record slide and animation timings, along with narrations, so the presentation will run through automatically.

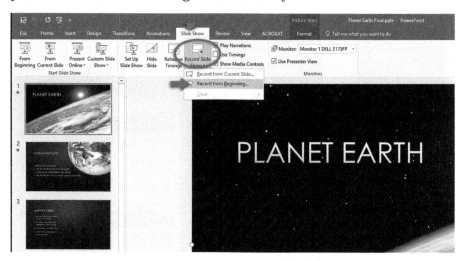

If you want to record narrations, click settings and make sure 'record audio' is checked and PowerPoint has found your microphone.

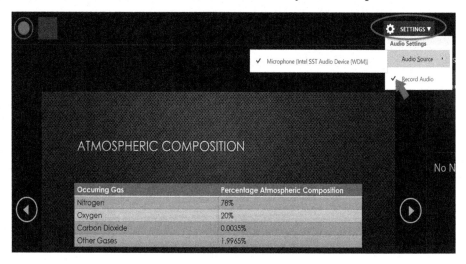

When you're ready, click the red button on the top left of the screen to start the recording.

Now give your presentation as if you were presenting to an audience, speaking into your microphone. It is best to be in a room where it is fairly quiet and with no echoes.

You can also use the screen annotation tools; draw on the slides, highlight points etc. PowerPoint will record your screen annotations, animations, bullets and transitions as you go through your presentation.

Once you are finished, click the stop button (large grey square on the top left).

**81**

# Export your Presentation

You can export your presentation as a video file and upload it to YouTube or social media. This will include all your slide timings, transitions, animations, as well as your narrations.

Click File, then select export.

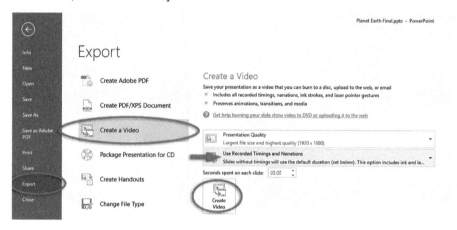

Set the presentation quality to the highest setting and select 'use recorded timings and narrations' to include your slide timings, annotations and narration recordings in the video.

Click 'create video', then select the folder you want to save it in. I'm saving my video in the 'videos' folder. Click 'save'.

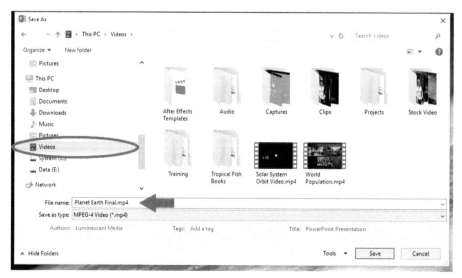

# Photo Albums

There are two ways you can create photo albums. You can use the album generator on the insert ribbon, or you can use a photo album template from office.com.

First, lets have a look at some of the templates available on office.com. Go to FILE and click NEW.

Type 'Photo Album' into the search field. You'll see a list of templates appear in the search results.

Double click on one of the template thumbnails to open a new presentation with that template.

Now you can start adding your images to the photo place holders in the presentation.

If there is a sample image already on the slide, to change it, right click and from the popup menu select 'change image'. From the slide out, select 'from file'. This is for photos stored on your computer.

On the slides, you'll see image place holders already laid out on the slides. To add an image, click the image icon in the middle.

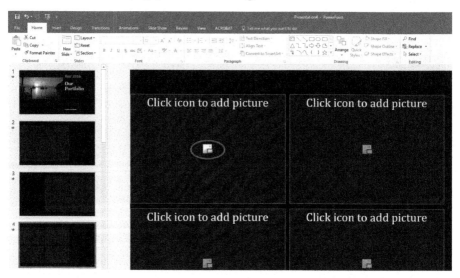

From the popup dialog box, select the image you want to insert. Do this with all the image place holders on all the slides.

You can also change the layouts of the photos. For example, on the second slide, say you wanted six small photos instead of one large photo.

To change the layout, click 'layout' from your home ribbon and select the layout from the drop down menu.

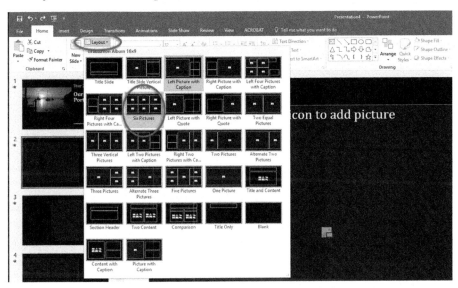

You can also add slide transitions as with ordinary slides, as well as animations for your photographs. To add animations, click your photo.

*If you want to select more than one photo, hold down your control key while you select your photos.*

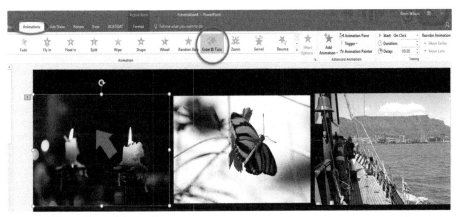

From the animations ribbon, select an animation pre set. Do this will all the images you want effects on.

You can also create a photo album using the album generator on the insert ribbon.

Go to your insert ribbon, and select 'photo album'.

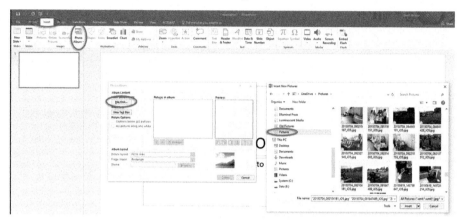

From the 'photo album' dialog box, click 'file/disk'. Then from the 'insert new pictures' dialog box, navigate to your pictures folder, or where your photos are stored, and click to select the ones you want. If you are selecting more than one photo, hold down the control key while you select your photos.

Click 'insert' when you're done.

You can also select a pre designed theme. To do this, click 'browse', then from the 'choose theme' dialog box, choose a theme from the list.

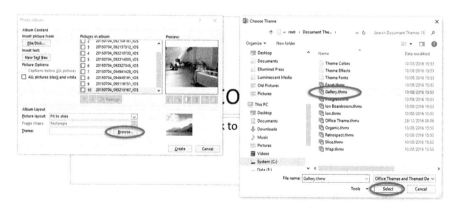

Click 'select' when you're done.

You can arrange the photos, one to a slide, more than one to a slide, or you can arrange to a slide with a title or caption.

To do this, click 'picture layout' and select an option. I'm going to select '1 picture with title'.

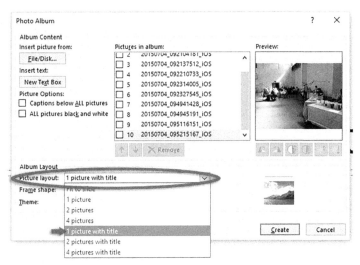

When you're done, click 'create'.

Now you can change the titles, add clipart and arrange the photos on your slides just like in any other PowerPoint presentation.

Edit your slides, add captions, headings and animations to your slides to make your album more exciting and interesting to watch.

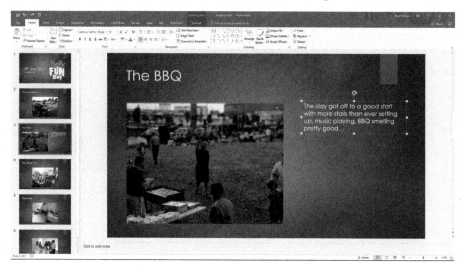

Run your photo album in the normal way. Press F5 on your keyboard.

# Chapter 5

# Giving Presentations

You have prepared your presentation and the time has come to present it to your audience.

In this chapter, we'll take a look at setting up your equipment in common scenarios using a projector and laptop, as well as examples on getting your presentation ready for presentation.

You can also present using a tablet PC if you have one and can make presenting to an audience easier.

We'll also take a look at broadcasting live and sending presentations online.

PowerPoint also allows you to create interactive exercises and questions with Office Mix. These are great for end of session quizzes or as homework for your class or group.

Lets begin by taking a look at a common setup.

# Setting Up

Connect your laptop to your projector. Modern projectors either use a VGA or an HDMI cable to connect. The projector in the example uses a VGA, but the principle is the same regardless of what cable you're using.

Connect the other end to your laptop

Plug the power lead into the projector.

Now fire up the projector. Once the projector is running, start up your laptop.

On your laptop, the best way to use PowerPoint is to use an extended screen display. This means that the projector screen is an extension of your laptop screen, rather than a duplicate. This will allow you to have notes and to see the next slides coming up in your presentation - the presenter display.

In Windows 10, to do this, hold down the windows key then tap 'P'. From the side panel that opens up, click 'extend'.

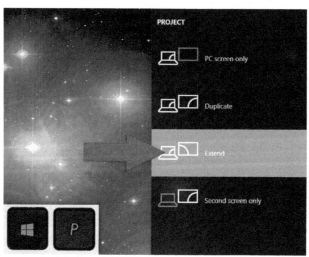

# Running your Presentation

The controls for running your presentation can be found on the slide show ribbon.

On the right hand side of the ribbon, click the drop down box next to 'monitor' and select the name/make of your second screen or projector.

This tells PowerPoint, which screen to display your presentation on for your audience to see. Your laptop or tablet screen is your presenter view. This will show you any notes you have written as well as the next slide. If you want this feature, tick 'use presenter view'.

To run your presentation, click 'from beginning' icon on the left hand side (or press F5). This will run your presentation from the first slide.

You have a few useful tools available while you present (circled in the image above).

You can zoom into a specific part of the slide to highlight it, by clicking the magnifying glass icon and positioning the rectangle over the part of the slide you want to show.

You can annotate your slides with notes to help your audience understand your point. Click the pen tool, select the pen and draw on the slide with your finger, a stylus or a mouse.

You can also present with a Windows 10 tablet running PowerPoint 2016 connected to a projector.

You may need a mini display port to VGA adapter, or a USB3 to VGA adapter to connect directly to the projector.

# Wireless Presenting

If you're using Windows 10, there is a feature that allows you to project to another Windows 10 device. So you could have your Windows 10 laptop hooked up to the projector and use your Windows 10 tablet to wirelessly project to your laptop.

Both your laptop and tablet will need to be on the same wireless network for this to work. Some laptops wont support this, but most modern ones do. To connect, on your tablet open your action centre and tap 'connect'.

Your Windows 10 tablet will scan the network for your laptop... In this demo, the laptop's network name is 'Asus-Laptop' and the tablet's name is 'surfaceone'.

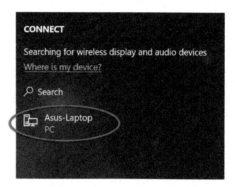

Once found, you'll see your laptop appear in the search results. Double tap on the name to connect.

On your laptop click 'yes' on the connection prompt that will appear on the bottom right of your screen.

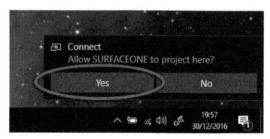

Once you click 'yes', you'll see a blue screen on your laptop while your devices connect.

If you're having trouble, make sure your laptop is set up to receive. Go to your settings icon on the start menu, click system, then click 'projecting to this PC'.

Projecting to this PC

Projecting to this PC

Project your Windows phone or PC to this screen, and use its keyboard, mouse and other devices, too.

Windows PCs and phones can project to this PC when you say it's OK

Available everywhere ⌄

Ask to project to this PC

Every time a connection is requested ⌄

Require PIN for pairing
◉⃝ Off .

This PC can only be discovered for projection when it is plugged in
◉ On

PC name    Asus-Laptop
Rename your PC

Make sure your laptop supports wireless projection, and that the settings are set up as shown in the screen above. Also check your wifi settings on your laptop and tablet.

Now you can start PowerPoint on your tablet and you'll see the screen project to the laptop.

With the laptop connected to your projector, you're all set to present with a wireless tablet.

You can now use PowerPoint on your tablet and run your presentation.

You can use the touch features on your tablet, such as a stylus and annotate your slides as you present.

# Present Online

You can set up a presentation and present it online, so anyone with a link to your presentation can 'tune in' and watch.

To do this, open your presentation and from the slideshow ribbon, click 'present online'.

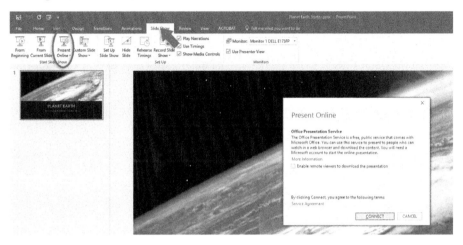

From the dialog box that appears, click 'connect'. *If you want your audience to be able to download a copy of your PowerPoint presentation, click the 'enable remove viewers to download the presentation'.*

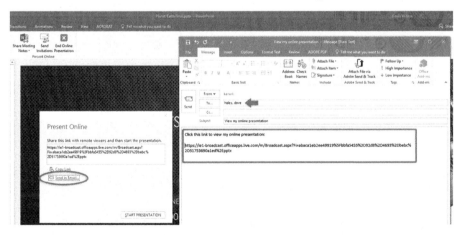

Next, invite the people you want to see your presentation. If you have Outlook 2016 installed on your machine, click 'send an email'. Add the email addresses to the email message that pops up. You can also click 'copy link' to copy to your clipboard and paste into sms/text message, imessage or skype.

## Chapter 5: Giving Presentations

When you are ready to begin, click 'start presentation' to begin your broadcast.

In the demonstration below, the laptop on the left is hosting the presentation.

The iPad and the Surface Tab are viewing the presentation in a web browser. These could be anywhere with an internet connection.

# Using Office Mix

Office Mix is a free add-on for Microsoft PowerPoint and is available to download from the following website.

mix.office.com

From the web page, click 'get office mix'.

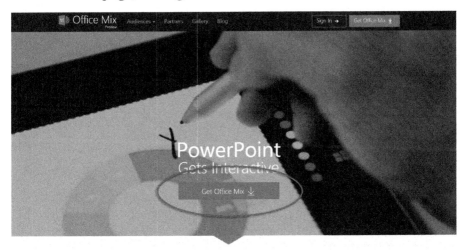

Click 'sign in with a Microsoft account', so mix is linked with your account you use for Microsoft Office.

If Microsoft Office was installed by your School, College or Work then select 'sign in with a work or school account'.

Sign in with your Microsoft Account email and password.

When prompted by your web browser, click 'save'.

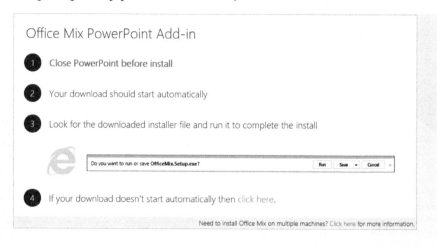

Then once the download has finished, click 'run'.

Click the check box to agree to the terms and conditions, then click 'install'.

Once the install has finished, you'll see a new ribbon in PowerPoint called mix.

With Office Mix you can add interactive elements such as quizzes. Tap the Office Mix ribbon and click 'Quizzes Videos Apps'.

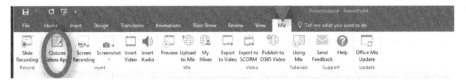

Click 'multiple choice quiz'. Click 'trust it' when prompted.

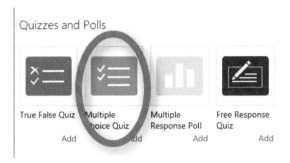

Start entering your questions and answers, as shown below.

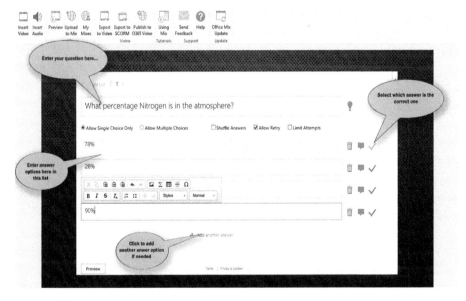

Insert another slide and add the multiple choice quiz as you did before. Carry on this until you have covered all your questions.

# Chapter 5: Giving Presentations

To publish the quiz to your students online. From the Mix ribbon, click 'upload to mix'

Click 'next', on the right hand side of the screen.

Login with your Microsoft Account

Click 'show me my mix' to open the published mix in your web browser. Enter the details as shown below.

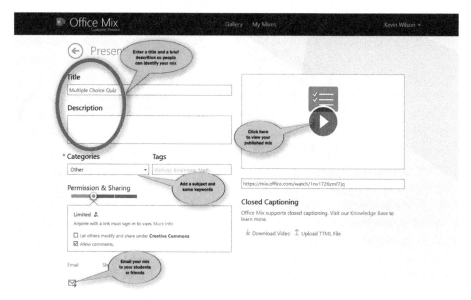

Set the permission level using the 'permission & sharing' slider. Private, means only you can see it. Limited, means anyone you send the link to and has a Microsoft Account. Unlisted, allows anyone you send a link to, to see it. Public, means your mix will appear in search results and in mix galleries. I'm leaving mine on limited for this example.

Click the email link to send your mix to your friends or students. They will receive an email with a link to click.

Click 'My Mixes' at the top of the screen. You can view your student's progress by clicking on 'Analytics'

From here you can view scores, questions they got right, ones they got wrong and overall progress.

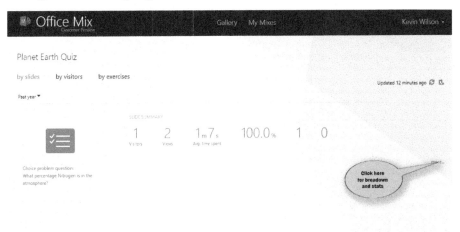

This is just one simple example. With Mix you can create presentations from your slides and record yourself and publish the whole thing online for friends to enjoy or colleagues to watch or even students to review a lecture etc.

You can do this by clicking 'slide recording' on the Mix ribbon. Start your presentation from the first slide, plug in your web cam and you can give your presentation and record yourself at the same time.

You can also record your screen, voice overs and export your presentation as a video file.

# Chapter 6

# Using PowerPoint Documents

In this section, we'll take a look at basic file management using OneDrive, Microsoft's cloud storage service. We'll get you started using OneDrive and how to manage and organise your files, so you can find your work easily.

You can also save presentations in different formats such as PDF or a video. We'll take a look at how this works, as well as printing slides, opening and saving PowerPoint presentations.

Also a look at online collaboration and explore how you can work on presentations together with colleagues and friends.

Lets begin by taking a look at some basic file management.

# OneDrive

OneDrive comes with Windows 10 and Microsoft Office and is probably the safest place to store all your files, as they are backed up in case your PC crashes.

You can see if OneDrive is set up, by clicking on OneDrive's icon in the system tray on the bottom right hand side of the screen.

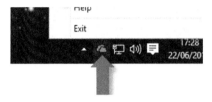

If it isn't there, click the small up arrow to reveal any hidden icons.

Click get started. Click the OneDrive icon.

Sign in with your Microsoft Account if prompted.

OneDrive will ask you where you want to store your OneDrive files on your computer while you work on them. Most of the time you can just leave it in it's default location. Click next.

OneDrive will scan for directories and files on your OneDrive account and ask you to copy them onto your local machine.

I usually select all of them. Click next.

The theory is, you work on the files on your local machine, edit, update, create save and do the things you need to do. Then OneDrive will copy these updates into your OneDrive Account on the Cloud, so you can access them from any of your devices such as tablet, phone or on the web. This is called synchronisation.

You can find all your files on OneDrive, by launching your File Explorer and scrolling down to the OneDrive section on the left hand side of the screen.

Now when you want to save your files from PowerPoint, save them into your OneDrive folder.

# Basic File Management

OneDrive already has a basic file structure for you to use. There is a documents folder for Word, Excel or PowerPoint documents; a folder for images and photographs; one for music, videos and a pubic folder for sharing.

You can move files from your OneDrive into the relevant folders. To do this, multiple select the documents, holding down the control key as you click document icons. Release the control key, click and drag the selected files to the folder.

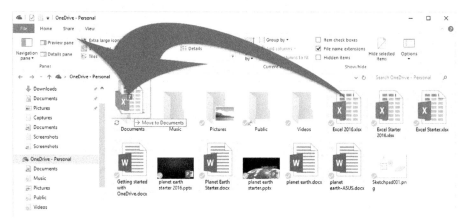

To create a new folder, eg one for PowerPoint only documents. Double click in the folder you want to create it in. In this example, I am going to create it in the documents folder.

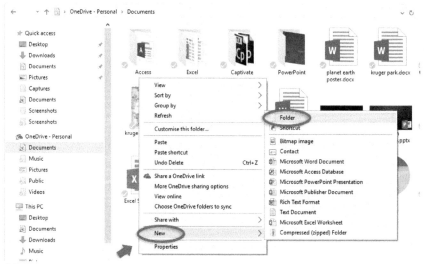

A new 'untitled' folder will appear, delete the text 'new folder' and type in a name.

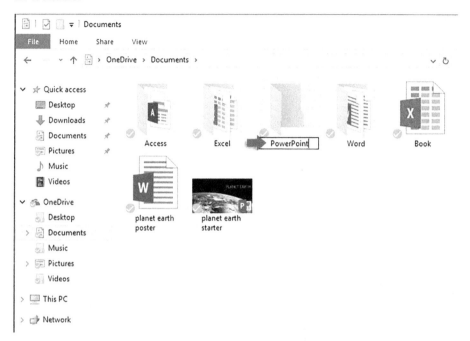

This folder will contain all the PowerPoint presentations, so an appropriate name would be 'PowerPoint'.

You can now select and drag all your PowerPoint presentations to this folder, and save any new ones directly into this folder.

# Opening a Saved Presentation

If PowerPoint is already open you can open previously saved presentations by clicking the FILE menu on the top left of your screen.

From the orange bar on the left hand side click 'open', then click 'OneDrive - Personal'.

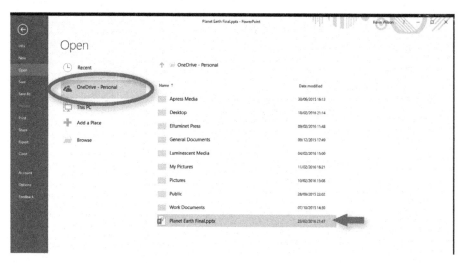

From the list, select the presentation you want to open. The presentation from the previous project was saved as 'planet earth.pptx', so this is the one I am going to open here.

For convenience, instead of searching thought your OneDrive, PowerPoint lists all your most recently opened Presentations. You can view these by clicking 'Recent' instead of 'OneDrive - Personal'.

Your latest files will be listed first.

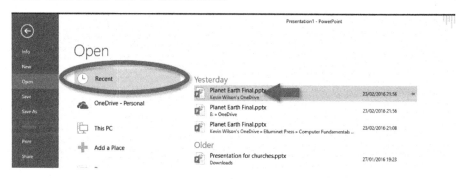

Double click the file name to open it.

# Saving your Presentation

Click the small disk icon on the top left of the screen. If this is a new presentation that hasn't been saved before, PowerPoint will ask you where you want to save it. Save all your work onto your OneDrive.

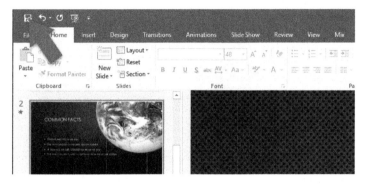

Click OneDrive Personal, then enter a name for your presentation in the field indicated by the red arrow below.

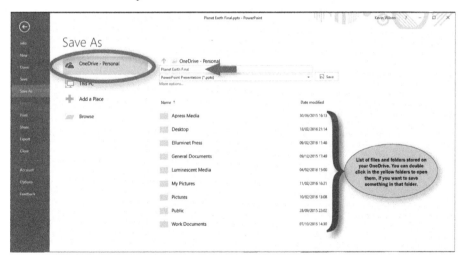

When you have done that click save.

# Save as a Different Format

To save your presentation in a different format, with your presentation open, click FILE.

From the backstage view, click 'Save As'.

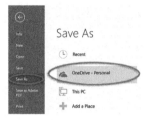

Select the folder you want to save your file in, eg, documents folder on your OneDrive.

Give your document a name, then underneath, click the down arrow and select a format. In this example, I am going to save the PowerPoint presentation as a PDF.

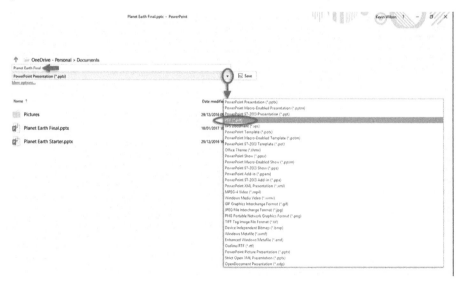

This is useful if you want to send a copy to someone that doesn't use Windows or have PowerPoint installed. Note with a PDF, you won't see all your animations or transitions in the file.

Click 'save' when you're done.

When you view the PDF version of your presentation, you'll see all the text and graphics.

You can also save as a video; either a MPEG4 video which is good for Macs, Windows, Tablets and Phones, or you can save as a Windows Media Video which will work on mostly Windows based machines.

If you save your presentation as a video, you'll get all your transitions and animations saved along with any timings and voice recordings you have done. If you haven't, you'll get the default timings for each slide transition and animation. The video presentation will run automatically, you won't be able to click to advance any slides etc.

# Print your Slides

To print your slides, click FILE on the top left hand corner of the screen, then select print.

In the screen below select the correct printer and number of copies you want.

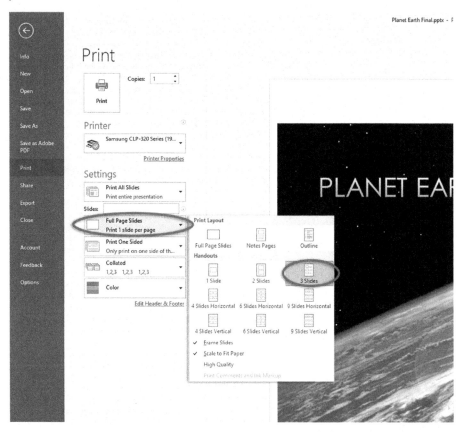

Then select how you want the slides to print out. Click where it says 'Full Page Slides'. 'Full Page Slides' prints out one slide per page and can be useful in some situations. If you are printing handouts, it makes sense to print more than one slide per page.

You'll see a pop up menu appear with some layout options for how to print out the slides on the page.

I usually select '3 slides', as it provides space for the audience to take notes on any particular slide.

You can then handout a copy of your slides to your audience so they can follow your presentation as you speak and take notes. I find this the most useful way to print slides.

If you just wanted the slides, you could also get six slides on a page. Just choose 'six horizontal slides' instead of '3 slides'.

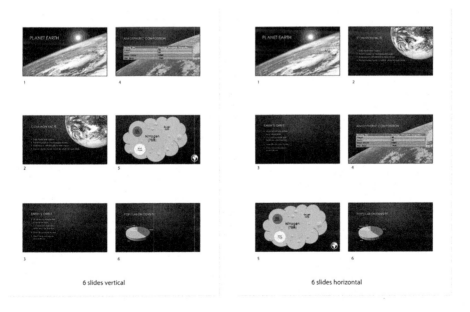

'Horizontal' means, the slides appear across the page rather than down the page. Notice how the slides are numbered above.

Sometimes it is useful to select 'black and white' or greyscale printing if you do not have a colour printer.

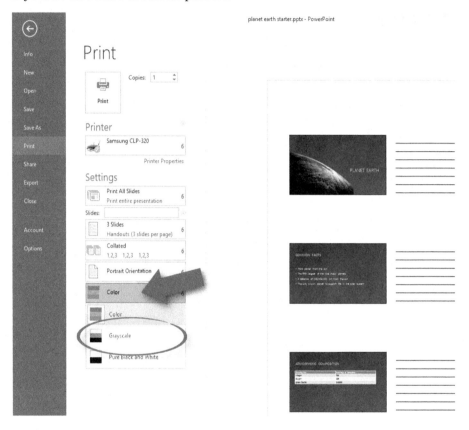

Click the print icon to print your presentation.

# Online Collaboration

A new feature that allows users to share their work with others. In the demo below, the user on the laptop has shared the PowerPoint presentation with the user on the tablet.

In the top right of PowerPoint's main screen, there is a share button. You can share any document you are working on with friends and colleagues.

If you want to share the presentation you are working on, click on the share button and enter their email address. Click the contacts icon next to the address field to add names from your contacts. Double click on each name in the address book list to add.

Select 'can edit' to allow people to make changes to your presentation. If you don't want people to make changes, change this option to 'can view'.

When the other person checks their email, on the tablet in this demonstration, they will receive a message inviting them to open the presentation you just shared.

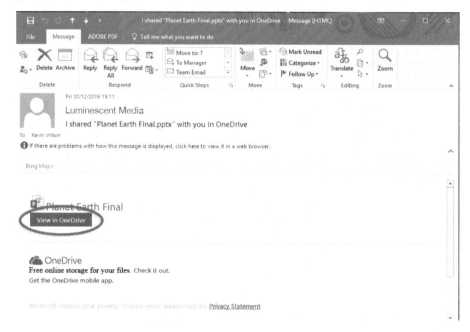

Click 'view in OneDrive', in the email message. The presentation will open in a web browser. Make sure you click 'sign in' on the top right of the screen and enter your Microsoft Account details when prompted.

Once you have signed in, click 'Edit Presentation', then click 'edit in PowerPoint'

This will download the document and open it up in PowerPoint 2016 installed on your computer (the tablet in this demo).

Here, the user on the tablet can start editing the presentation. As an example, they're going to add a bullet point to the list.

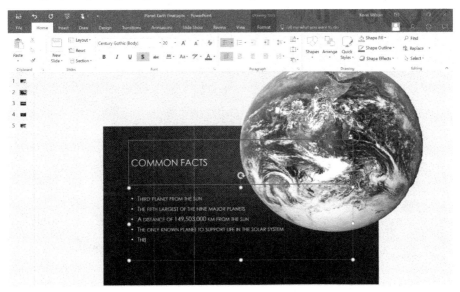

You'll be able to see who is editing what, indicated with a user icon on the top right of the text boxes, circled below.

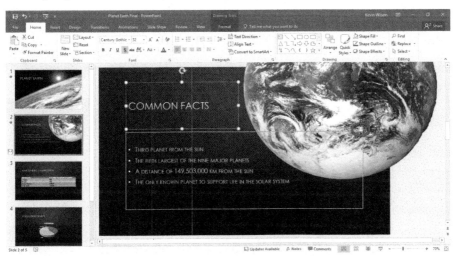

We can see here on the laptop screen, that the user on the tablet is editing the bottom text box.

# Normal View

Normal view is the default view and the best way to design and develop your presentation. It lists all your slides down the left hand side, with the selected slide displayed in the centre of the screen for you to work on.

# Outline View

The outline view, shows you a list of your slide's text, rather than a thumbnail view of the slide. You wont see any images or graphics inserted into any of your slides on the left hand side.

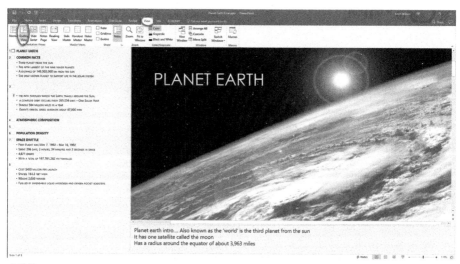

# Slide Sorter View

The slide sorter view shows you a thumbnail list of all your slides in the presentation.

As the name suggests, it allows you to easily see all your slides and makes it easier for you to put them into the correct order.

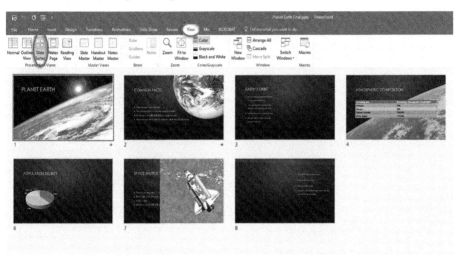

As well as hide certain slides you may not need in a particular session when presenting. To do this, right click the slide, then from the popup menu select 'hide slide'.

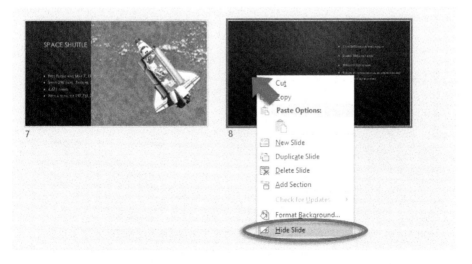

Hidden slides are greyed out with the slide number crossed out. To un-hide the slide, right click on the slide, and click 'hide slide' again.

**123**

# Note Page View

Note page view, allows you to see the slide with the notes associated with that slide. Makes it easier to add notes to each slide. Or to review notes already added to a slide.

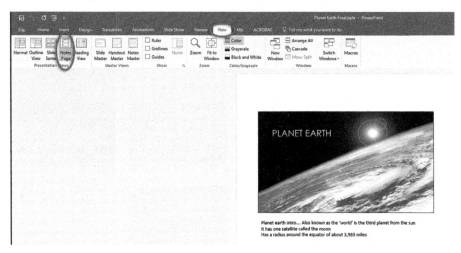

# Reading View

This view allows you to play your PowerPoint presentation slideshow within the PowerPoint window.

# Chapter 6: Using PowerPoint Documents

# Index

**D**

**E**

**F**

**G**

**H**

**I**

**L**

# Index

CPSIA information can be obtained
at www.ICGtesting.com
Printed in the USA
LVOW06s2348070517
533589LV00033B/271/P